TOTALLY
ORCHIDS

To my mother, Marianne, who taught me to see,
and my father, Robert, who taught me to hear.

Celestial Arts Publishing
P.O. Box 7123
Berkeley, CA 94707

Cover design and illustration: Bob Greisen
Interior design and typesetting: Susan Hernday
Interior illustrations: Carolyn Vibbert

Totally Orchids is produced by becker&mayer!, Ltd.

Printed in Singapore

ISBN 0-89087-782-3
Library of Congress Catalog Card Number: 95-71814

First Printing, 1996

1 2 3 4 / 99 98 97 96

Other books in the Totally Flowers series:
Totally Sunflowers
Totally Roses
Totally Tulips

TOTALLY ORCHIDS

by Rob Cardillo

Illustrated by
Carolyn Vibbert

CELESTIAL ARTS
BERKELEY, CALIFORNIA

CONTENTS

A MISUNDERSTOOD BEAUTY

Primitive and mysterious, orchids have aroused passions and piqued curiosities for centuries. People of ancient cultures were fascinated with them, and made magical potions from orchid roots. Orchid hunters in the New World made fortunes and lost lives seeking new plants for their wealthy patrons.

Early growers spent decades studying the cryptic habits of orchids. Unfortunately, over time the intense interest in these wondrous plants has led to many misconceptions—including some that persist to this day. Among the greatest myths are that orchids are expensive to buy, difficult to grow, and need expert greenhouse care. Not any more. If you can raise African violets or maintain a tropical fish tank, you should have few problems growing and enjoying orchids wherever you live.

HISTORY

EARLY SEX SYMBOLS

The Father of Botany, Theophrastus (372-287 B.C.) noted orchids in his catalog of healing plants. As ancient medicine was often based on similarities between plant forms and human anatomy, the Mediterranean *orchis* plant was named for its water-storage organ which resembles human testicles. In turn, the Greeks believed elixirs made from orchid roots would serve as aphrodisiacs or cure various sexual problems. Other early herbalists thought orchids were the food of satyrs—lecherous goat-like gods who rambled about the woods—and referred to them as Satyrion. As orchid seeds are nearly invisible, some cultures believed that the flowers arose from the spilled semen of copulating animals.

ASIAN ROOTS

Early Eastern scholars found orchids of interest as well, but more for the beauty of their flowers, foliage, and scent than for their medicinal qualities. They were referred to in the *I Ching* almost twenty-five hundred years ago. Confucius thought the orchid flower to be an ideal metaphor for the enlightened man and its heady fragrance a sign of brotherhood. One orchid, *Cymbidium ensifolium*, has been continually cultivated in China for more than two thousand years. Both Chinese and Japanese artists revered orchids, and their graceful blooms and fine foliage became the subjects of many paintings.

EUROPEAN INTRODUCTIONS

Although orchids are found on every continent, colorful tropical specimens came to the West by way of the explorers and missionaries that sailed the globe in the 1700s. Naturalists throughout Europe sought botanical and zoological curiosities from the New World; and by 1789 a handful of orchids were growing under glass at The Royal Botanical Gardens at Kew. Famous seamen such as James Cook and William Bligh claimed exotic orchids as part of their booty from newly discovered lands.

Son Flower

John Parkinson, in THEATRUM BOTANICUM, *published in 1640, reports that a man would "begat men children" if he ate a large orchid tuber.*

Unusual Crossings

During their long sea voyage, most orchids perished in the dank holds of the great sailing ships, but at least one traveled first-class—a flowering *Oncidium* from South America made the journey to England hanging in the captain's cabin. Other orchids arrived quite by accident—roots of *Cattleya labiata* were used as packing material in a shipment from Brazil and were later rejuvenated by (and named for) William Cattley. The blooms from this species were so spectacular that demand soared for new orchids and collecting expeditions were immediately dispatched to South America.

Orchidmania

Orchids became an obsession for wealthy Victorians during the 1800s. Their exotic and curious blooms, high prices, and need for heated conservatories appealed to the status-conscious upper classes, and new shipments from overseas were received with great excitement. As orchidmania (or orchidelirium) hit Europe full force in 1850, collecting trips became ruthlessly competitive. Tens of thousands of one species would be taken to ensure an exclusive market. The few survivors were auctioned off to enthusiasts who would have to pay outrageous sums for a single plant. Acres of rain forest were felled to collect the orchids clinging to the treetops. Records of where plants came from were often falsified or kept secret to prevent other collectors from gaining any advantage. Collectors faced dis-

ease, insects, hostile natives, and death as
they penetrated deeper and deeper into tropical jungles in search of the next magnificent
bloom.

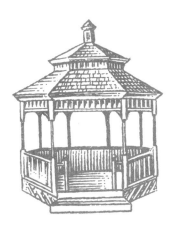

GROWING PAINS

As new orchids arrived, European horticulturists placed them in orangeries—fire-heated greenhouses where orange trees were kept—but the dry heat tolerated by the citrus killed most orchid specimens. Further experiments with steam heat, ventilation systems, and misting schedules were a little more successful. Still, the secret of propagating orchids from seed eluded growers for another hundred years.

Orchid Warning!

"The roots are to be used with discretion....They are hot and moist in operation, under the dominion of Venus, and provoke lust exceedingly which the dried and withered roots do restrain."

—CULPEPER, *writing in* BRITISH HERBAL

Orchids Today

Unfortunately, many of the famed European orchid collections perished during the First and Second World Wars due to the lack of heating fuel. Collections in the United States, however, thrived. California and Florida soon became the new orchid capitals. Methods to create striking hybrids were perfected and this, along with the discovery of more tolerant species from the wild, resulted in a phenomenal number of orchids for sale—many at very reasonable prices. Today, commercial growers in Asia air ship millions of blooms to florists' shops around the globe, and orchid-growing has become a most seductive hobby.

BOTANY

The most difficult task facing any budding orchid fan is deciphering the intimidating vocabulary that surrounds this horticultural hobby. Long Latin names, strange abbreviations, and technical terms are discouraging for most novice growers and can easily dampen initial excitement. To confuse things more, most of the more than 100,000 orchids have no common names and must be referred to entirely by scientific nomenclature. Taking time to become familiar with basic orchid botany and terminology will help you to grow and appreciate these most unusual plants.

TREE HUGGERS

In nature, most orchids are "epiphytes," which means they grow on top of other plants. Strong and rope-like, epiphytic roots hold the orchid plant firmly onto branches, trunks, or vines; but unlike parasites, they take no food from their host. These aerial roots absorb needed moisture from the air and nutrients washed down from decaying materials above. A spongy, silvery material called "velamen" covers and protects these exposed roots from intense sunlight and helps the plant retain moisture during dry spells. A few orchids grow on rocks rather than trees and are known as "lithophytes." The remaining orchids live a more typical herbaceous existence, with fine roots growing into good old terra firma. These are known as "terrestrial" orchids.

WAY TO GROW

Orchids grow in two distinct ways. "Sympodial" orchids send out new growth horizontally from the base of the plant, similar to a bearded iris. Often, sympodial orchids have thick and fleshy stems called "pseudobulbs" that are used for water storage. "Monopodial" orchids produce new growth vertically from the top of the plant.

Graveyard Ghouls

Although no orchids are parasites, at least one is carnivorous. The hollow bulbs of Schomburgkia tibicinus *are home to colonies of native ants who use neighboring bulbs as graveyards. The orchid feeds off the corpses by sending a root through the adjacent bulb's entrance.*

FLORAL SECRETS

All orchid flowers are constructed from the same basic parts. However, the size, shape, and color of these parts vary tremendously from species to species, resulting in a dizzying array of floral permutations. Some orchids produce a single flower, others bloom in masses—but all orchid flowers have three sepals, three petals, and a lip, which is also known as the "labellum." The lip is the most variable feature of the orchid flower, and can take the form of a little frill, a liquid-filled pouch, or even an insect which attracts pollinators.

POLLINATION

Orchids rely on insects for pollination, and use nectar to lure them to their blooms. Some orchids, however, have developed strange ways of ensuring their pollen is moved from flower to flower. When a bee lands on the lip of the bucket orchid, *Coryanthes speciosa*, it slips into a pouch of intoxicating liquid and struggles out another opening lined with pollen. Other orchids rely on a spring-loaded system to catapult their gluey pollen onto any insects that visit their blooms. A few species emit the odors of goats or rotting meat to attract flies, and some entice moths with their nocturnal perfumes.

Many orchid flowers even look like the insects they need for pollination. Several *Oncidium* orchids produce dangling, bee-like blooms that antagonize real bees into butting their flowers, thereby ensuring pollination. The bee orchid, *Trichoceros parviflorus*, looks and smells so much like a female bee that males attempt to mate with the flower.

Orchid Ice Cream?

Most ice cream lovers don't know this, but one of their favorite flavors comes from an orchid—notably Vanilla planifolia. *A vining species from Central America, this orchid can climb to seventy-five feet or more and produces hundreds of seedpods that are known as vanilla beans. Once an important crop for export, it has largely been replaced by artificial vanilla.*

The Name Game

Like all life on our planet, orchids have two Latin names to indicate their genus and species. The "genus" name (plural "genera") always comes before the "species" name, and has the first letter capitalized. The species name follows in lowercase type and is often a descriptive term. Hence *Cattleya bicolor* was named for its two-toned flowers and *Angraecum philippinense* was first found in the Philippines. Native orchids, untouched by breeders, are known as species orchids. Often endangered from over-collecting, most species orchids are now grown in commercial greenhouses.

HYBRIDS

When horticulturists began cross-breeding different wild orchids, hybrids were created. Although hybrids are uncommon in nature and are often infertile or unhealthy, orchids hybridize very readily and usually produce robust offspring. Taking advantage of this natural promiscuity, breeders began creating hybrids with dramatically enhanced flowers, compact foliage, increased vigor, and dozens of other desired qualities. Today, there are more than 100,000 orchid hybrids registered, and thousands more released each year.

Hybrids created between two orchid species are often given a "grex," or group, name. Grex names are always in Roman type with the first letter capitalized. For instance, all the crosses between *Paph. delenatii* and *Paph. laevigatum* are called by their grex name,

Paph. Delphi. Within a grex or species, plants with exceptional qualities are distinguished as "cultivars" or varieties. Cultivar names, always written within single quotation marks, often have less serious-sounding names—for example, 'Volcano', 'Splendiferous', and 'Her Majesty' are cultivar names. The pedigree or parentage of a hybrid is often listed in parentheses after its name.

Hybrid Hysteria

When John Lindley was shown the first hybrid in 1856, he exclaimed, "You will drive the botanists mad!"

Intergeneric Names

Early botanists, surprised that orchids of two different genera could be crossed, needed a new name for the offspring. At first, these intergeneric hybrids were named by blending the two genus names together. Thus when a *Sophronitis* and a *Cattleya* were crossed, the hybrid offspring was called *Sophrocattleya*. It logically followed that when *Sophrocattleya* was crossed with a *Laelia*, the result was called *Sophrolaeliocattleya*. When yet a further cross involving a *Brassavola* was produced, the famed orchidist E. A. Bowles wisely suggested creating artificial genus names, in this case *Potinara*, to prevent any further tongue twisting.

Genus Abbreviations

Because genus names of many orchids are so long, they are conveniently abbreviated:

B. = *Brassavola*

Bc. = *Brassocattleya*

Blc. = *Brassolaeliocattleya*

Bro. = *Broughtonia*

Brs. = *Brassia*

Cat. or *C.* = *Cattleya*

Cym. = *Cymbidium*

Den. = *Dendrobium*

Enc. = *Encyclia*

Epi. = *Epidendrum*

L. = *Laelia*

Lc. = *Laeliocattleya*

Milt. = *Miltonia*

Odont. = *Odontoglossum*
Onc. = *Oncidium*
Paph. = *Paphiopedilum*
Phal. = *Phalaenopsis*
Pot. = *Potinara*
Sc. = *Sophrocattleya*
Slc. = *Sophrolaeliocattleya*
V. = *Vanda*

GROWING ORCHIDS

Many orchids make great house-plants and will faithfully unfurl their flowers year after year. Unlike ferns and philodendrons, orchids play by their own rules. They still need light, heat, food, and water—but in different ways and amounts than most other plants. The secret to happy, healthy orchids is to become aware of how orchids survive in the wild. Start "thinking" like an orchid and the special considerations they require will become logical. As a bonus, you'll find most orchids forgiving of poor growing conditions; and most will linger a long while before dying. This natural resiliency gives you plenty of time to correct any problems and enjoy their blooms again.

LIGHT

Clinging to tree trunks high in the rain forest canopy, orchids are surrounded by an abundance of bright, filtered light, while still being sheltered from the cruel tropical sun. Other orchids live in shadier areas nearer the jungle floor. Because of these differences, orchids are often categorized by their light requirements— high, medium, or low—and it's helpful to know which your particular growing area can provide before shopping for plants. To check if your plants are getting the right amount of light, examine the foliage. Dark green leaves, spindly growth, and no flowers are signals of too little light. White or scorched leaves indicate too much light. Orchid leaves receiving the right level of illumination will usually be a light, grassy green.

TEMPERATURE

Orchids adapted to the cooler climes of mountaintops have different needs than those living in the warmer lowlands. Accordingly, orchids are divided into three temperature ranges—cool, intermediate, and warm—depending on their tropical origins. Although it's easy to keep cool and intermediate, or intermediate and warm orchids together, it would be a challenge to keep cool and warm species happy in the same environment. As a rule of thumb, intermediate-temperature orchids require a minimum nighttime temperature of 55 degrees F and should do well in most North American homes. Cooler species prefer a drop to 50 degrees F and may do better in the Northeast or Northwest, while warmer species favor a drop to only 60 degrees F and are best suited to more tropical areas of the country.

You can buy a maximum-minimum thermometer to track your home temperature ranges, but keep in mind that specific temperatures are not as critical for flowering as the need for a nighttime drop of at least 10 to 15 degrees F.

Wall-to-Wall Orchids

It's been estimated that a single seedpod of the swan orchid, Cycnoches chlorochilon, contains 3,770,000 seeds! If they all matured, the earth would be blanketed with orchids in just four generations.

WATER

In their native homes, most orchids are perched high up on tree trunks with their roots freely exposed to air. During the short tropical downpours, the roots are drenched but dry out quickly. Unlike other plants, orchid roots are not accustomed to contact with water for any length of time. In fact, one of the quickest ways to kill an orchid is by overwatering and allowing the roots to suffocate in waterlogged soil.

So when do you water? No hard and fast rules apply. Watering depends on the age and type of species, dryness of your house, size and type of pot, soil mix, and so forth. Your best bet is to lift the plant and feel its weight. When it's too light, water. If you're in doubt, wait a few days. And when you do water, water thoroughly and early in the day to allow the foliage time to dry. Keep the water off the leaves as much as possible to discourage any swimming pools for bacteria or fungi. An easy way to do this is to immerse the entire pot up to its rim in a bucket of tepid water for a few minutes. Many experienced growers prefer filtered water or rainwater for their prized specimens, but unsoftened tap water is usually adequate.

Food

Wild orchids are light feeders and are almost entirely nourished by bits of bird droppings and leaves that wash down the trunks to become trapped in their roots. Liquid plant food diluted to one-third strength and given once a week is usually adequate for their well-being. This "weakly, weekly" feeding is fine for most species, but watch for a buildup of white residue on the soil surface. If this occurs, you'll need to periodically flush the soil with lots of water to wash away the mineral salts. Some growers prefer the organic approach and use liquid fish emulsion instead of chemical plant food. Orchids (as well as cats) seem to love it and it leaves no soil residue. Generally, orchids require more nourishment during their growing season, and less when they are dormant.

Air and Humidity

Imagine the air in the jungle just after a rainstorm when balmy, buoyant breezes are blowing through the trees. This fresh, moist atmosphere is what growers try to re-create for optimal orchid performance. Most homes are too dry for orchids—especially in the winter and with hot-air heating systems. One easy way to create a more humid environment around your plants is to place the pots on top of gravel- or stone-filled trays to which a little water is added periodically. These trays, which are available commercially or can be made at home, create a humid microclimate around the orchid plants, while keeping their roots from touching the water. A simple plant mister is also an effective way to raise the humidity for a short while. Ideally, relative humidity should be at least 50 percent, and experienced growers can sense when the air is too dry. You can also monitor the relative humidity in your home with an inexpensive hygrometer. Good air circulation is also critical for orchid health. Stagnant, damp air will only encourage bacteria and fungus attacks, and your plants may burn during the summer if there isn't a breeze to cool them. Keep a nearby window open or buy a small fan and direct it just above or below your tropical babies.

Not for Windowsills

Grammatophyllum speciosum *is the world's largest orchid. One plant can weigh up to a ton and produce eight-foot flower stems of fifty flowers each.*

Orchids by the Window

Windowsills are where most orchid collections begin. Try using a southern or eastern window with a wide sill to prevent the plant foliage from touching the glass in winter. If the light is too intense for your orchids, move the plant away from the window or hang a sheer curtain to reduce the intensity. If there isn't enough light, move your orchids to a sunnier sill or use reflective boards to bounce some of the ambient light back toward the plants. Orchids kept over the kitchen sink or in the bathroom have the additional benefit of extra humidity. Choose specimens with low light needs, such as *Phalaenopsis* or *Paphiopedilum*.

Orchids Under Lights

Window light does have its limitations. Although many orchids will do well on a bright windowsill, you can't control the number and length of sunny days. That's when orchid growers turn to artificial light. Inexpensive shop-type fluorescent fixtures produce an abundance of cool light without running up your electric bill. Place the fixtures so that the bulbs are about six to eight inches above the plant leaves and use a timer to keep them lit for about fifteen hours a day. If you want to grow orchids that require even more light, you'll need a high-intensity discharge (HID) fixture. Although these units cost hundreds of dollars initially, their giant bulbs can provide enough light for dozens of sun-hungry species.

ORCHIDS OUTDOORS

Some lucky gardeners in Florida, California, and Hawaii can grow orchids outdoors all year round. For the rest of us, we can at least afford giving our prized plants a vacation on the patio. A summer outing means greater air movement, rainwater treatments, and more sun—all of which can rejuvenate sickly specimens. Allow your orchids time to adjust to the great outdoors by first placing them in shady nooks and gradually weaning them to sunnier spots. If the leaves begin to scorch, move them back toward the shade. Keep the pots off the ground and you'll increase air circulation and make the foliage a little harder for the slugs and snails to find. When it's time to bring your orchids in, spend a few minutes with each plant and check for insects. If you treat problems now, you'll stop them before they have a chance to spread indoors.

Pots and Containers

Many orchids whose ancestors thrived on jungle branches are actually quite content to live in special orchid pots that feature large drainage holes. Naturally, to keep their roots from becoming waterlogged, saucers are never used under these pots. Pots made from clay or plastic are available in a wide range of sizes. Clay pots allow better aeration of the roots and give a little more stability, but plastic pots separate from roots more easily when you're repotting and can endure a few minor bumps.

Pots aren't the only places to grow your orchids. Slatted baskets made of rot-resistant wood such as cedar, teak, or redwood are great for orchids whose flowers tend to drape downward. These hanging baskets have the added bonus of freeing up some shelf space.

Some orchids prefer being "real" epiphytes. Their bare roots are tied or stapled to hanging slabs of oak bark. This technique is known as "plaquing" or "rafting." Often, a small piece of moss or other absorbent material is placed between the roots and the slab to retain moisture. These bark slabs last for years and allow the roots plenty of room to breathe. Because the roots are exposed, they will need more frequent watering.

Air Fresheners

A NASA scientist has added orchids to the list of houseplants that purify air. Experiments with Dendrobium *orchids proved that the plants remove acetone, methyl alcohol, and ethyl acetate—all chemicals released when people exhale.*

POTTING MIXES

Standard potting soils should never be used with orchids. Mixes suitable for houseplants hold too much moisture, and that will cause orchid roots to suffocate and rot. Use special orchid potting mixes instead. These blends drain quickly and allow good aeration while still providing an adequate foothold for the roots. Most mixes contain chunks of fir tree bark in various sizes, along with other inert substances such as sphagnum moss, tree fibers, charcoal, and perlite, depending on the blend. Professional orchidists tailor their mixes to individual species and situations, but beginners should stay with a medium blend for epiphytes and a finer blend for terrestrials.

Repotting

Sooner or later your orchids will need repotting. Repotting is necessary when either the roots are growing over the sides (in sympodial orchids) or when the potting mixture has decomposed to the point that it's smothering the roots. You can tell if the mix has rotted too much by digging down an inch or so. If the soil is black and mushy, it's time to repot. If the plant moves easily when jiggled, the roots may already be rotting, and repotting should take place immediately. Unless it's an emergency, schedule your repotting for the period just after bloom time. This is when new growth begins and the plant can re-establish itself quickly.

Begin by removing the orchid from its old pot by gently tapping the bottom. If the root-ball won't budge, soak the pot in tepid water for an hour and try again. Remove and discard as much of the old compost as possible, and trim any brown or soft ends of the roots. Often you can simply repot the plant back into its original container, but when you need a larger pot, don't make too big a jump in size—excess soil retains too much water. Work on a clean surface and rinse new pots with a diluted bleach solution to kill any bacterial or viral contaminants. Fill one-third of the new pot with stones, pot shards, or plastic foam peanuts. Stones and shards are good for top-heavy plants that need stabilizing.

If the plant is sympodial, place the old growth to one side and aim the new growth toward the center of the pot. For monopodial plants, center the roots. Hold the orchid in its new pot and add dry orchid potting mix around the roots. Shake and tap the pot to settle the new soil. If the root system is weak, support the plant with a small stake. Water thoroughly, but then don't water again for three weeks. Keep the humidity high with frequent mistings.

The Orchid Underground

One orchid lives entirely underground. The Australian Rhizanthelle gardneri *has no chlorophyll or roots, and feeds entirely on a thread-like fungus that surrounds dead tree stumps. It bears a small red-and-yellow flower that never sees daylight.*

Orchids From Divisions

Most mature sympodial orchids can be divided when they're dormant by simply cutting the plant apart with a sharp, sterile knife, leaving at least three pseudobulbs per division. Once they're cut, you can pull apart the roots and replant each division into a new pot. "Backbulbs"—old pseudobulbs that don't produce new leaves—can also be removed and repotted for additional plants.

Monopodial orchids will sometimes produce "keikis," little plantlets that form on the flower stem. Once these baby plants sprout roots, they can be cut off and started on their own. You can also cut off and repot the top of a tall monopodial orchid and get two plants from one.

Orchids From Seed

Early attempts at raising orchids from their dust-like seeds were frustrating. The few plants that actually did grow frequently died before blooming. In 1899, a French botanist discovered that a microscopic fungus was needed for healthy germination. In 1930, a formula was developed that replaced the need for the fungus, and orchidists everywhere began propagation in earnest. Growing orchids from seed at home is difficult, but not impossible. Many companies offer amateurs a "flasking" service where you may send your seeds to be planted in a sterile medium. They are returned to you later as seedlings.

MERICLONING

Since the 1960s, a sophisticated method of propagation known as "meristem cloning" ("mericloning" for short) has produced outstanding results. Mericlones are genetically identical plants created by culturing bits of growing embryonic tissue from a valued specimen. The tissues grow in nutrient-filled laboratory flasks, and are later transplanted into small pots. This technique allows breeders to create hundreds of exact genetic copies of a single, prized hybrid.

PROBLEMS

It's no secret that healthy orchid plants are better able to resist insects and diseases than plants that are stressed. The easiest way to prevent stress is by watering properly and watching humidity. Too much water or humidity damages orchid roots and allows disease spores to propagate. Too little water or humidity invites insect attacks. To keep your plants healthy, learn the warning signs of improper watering, inadequate light, or inappropriate temperatures and correct them as soon as possible.

Poor hygiene can also affect orchid health. Viruses are easily transmitted throughout a collection and, once established, there is no cure. Symptoms include deformed flowers and irregular streaking patterns in leaves. To prevent a viral outbreak, sterilize your tools with alcohol or by passing metal blades over a flame before each use. Keep working surfaces clean and wash your hands frequently when repotting.

Pests that threaten orchids include:

- Scales are tiny nonmoving, helmet-shaped insects. There are two types—hard and soft—and they are usually due to overly dry conditions. Remove them with an alcohol-soaked swab, and increase humidity by misting more often.
- Spider mites are nearly invisible, spider-like insects that leave tiny holes in leaves. Look for fine spider webs in hot, dry conditions. Wash leaves with a mild soap solution and mist with water daily to discourage their return.

- Mealy bugs are cottony creatures that like to hide in the crevices of stems and leaves, particularly in stressed or dry plants. Remove with alcohol-soaked swabs and raise humidity by misting.
- Slugs and snails are mostly a nocturnal problem of outdoor orchids. Pick off individuals and sprinkle diatomaceous earth on the surface of the soil. Diatomaceous earth contains the silicified skeletons of planktonic algae and is available at garden stores. Destroy daytime hiding areas under moist decaying matter.
- Aphids are small soft-bodied, slow-moving insects that are found in groups near tender new growth. Wash them off with mild soapy water or alcohol swabs.

USING ORCHIDS

ORCHID DECOR

Orchids make great cut flowers, some blooms lasting for weeks with occasional mistings. A single flowering spike in a simple vase can create a striking minimalist arrangement that complements any decor. Don't be shy about removing the bloom—cutting the flower allows the plant greater recovery time for next year's display. For best results, make sure the flowers are fully open for at least two weeks before you cut. Using a sterile razor, slice the stem on a diagonal. Keep the vase water fresh and periodically trim the stem, especially if it's soft or discolored. Mix in a few greens to soften the arrangement and keep top-heavy flowers from toppling the vase by using a frog (a small florist's weight) in the bottom.

CORSAGES AND MORE

Why not wear your favorite orchids? When special occasions arise and your cherished *Cattleya* or *Phalaenopsis* is in bloom, you can create your own corsage, bouquet, or boutonniere. Cut the flower stem at the base of the plant with a sterilized razor. Trim the stem to the appropriate length and wrap it with thin, stiff wire. For a quick boutonniere, simply cover the wire with a wrapping of dark green florist's tape. Combine two or three wire-wrapped blooms with bits of fern, ivy, or ribbon to create a unique corsage or bouquet. Always finish up by wrapping florist's tape around the stems to hide the wire. To prolong the life of your arrangement, stick the stem ends in tiny glass water vials (another florist's item) or wrap them in damp cotton before taping. Refrigerate in a bag or box.

Photographing Orchids

Flower photos are pretty, but orchid close-ups are hypnotizing. The intense colors and patterns of their sculpted faces make them the perfect subject to explore with your camera. To get the best shots, use a close-focusing macro lens on your tripod-mounted camera. Place the orchid in a light that's bright but diffused and with no hard shadows. Many photographers use a colored background to simplify and complement the flower. Use a fine-grained film, a cable release, and focus carefully. Bracket your shots by one or two f-stops if you're using slide film, and always allow extra exposure for white or light-colored flowers.

CHOOSING ORCHIDS

THE RIGHT ORCHID FOR YOU

There are more than 25,000 wild orchid species, and more than four times that number of hybrids. With that many choices, how can you possibly decide which beauties to bring into your home? First, look at the growing conditions you can provide. Are you limited to a bright, warm windowsill or are you setting up lights in a cool basement? Do you live in sunny Florida or chilly Minnesota? How much time and money do you have to devote to your newly adopted friends? To help you decide which orchid is best for you, let's look briefly at eight popular genera.

CATTLEYA

Named for William Cattley, the British horticulturist who discovered the first *Cattleya* when it was used as packing material for a shipment of plants from the New World. The original corsage flower, cattleyas are one of the easiest and most popular orchids grown. Big, showy blossoms and fleshy pseudobulbs are trademarks of this genus. These pseudobulbs tolerate periods of drought well, but overwatering can damage them quickly. They enjoy strong diffused light, and will prosper in bright windows or under fluorescent fixtures. Mini-catts, better suited for windowsill growing, are becoming more available. Cattleyas are divided into two groups—unifoliate and bifoliate—depending on whether they have one or two leaves per pseudobulb. Unifoliates have a few large flowers, while bifoliates develop smaller but more numerous waxy blooms. They are native to Central and South America.

SELECTIONS

C. aurantiaca—a small bifoliate plant with drooping clusters of three to twelve bright orange flowers—some with brown or purple markings. It is native to Central America and widely used in breeding. Keep on the dry side, but don't let pseudobulbs shrivel.

C. bowringiana—a robust lithophyte from Belize. The large, fat pseudobulbs produce up to twenty small deep rose flowers with dark lips and whitish throats. Requires more water than other catts. A pale form is grown that is almost blue.

C. labiata—a widely grown orchid with large seven-inch velvety, rose-colored flowers. Each bloom has a tiny ruffled lip with two orange spots. Flowers are fragrant and long-lasting. This two-foot-tall unifoliate comes from Brazil. The *alba* form is pure white.

C. skinneri—the national flower of Costa Rica, and very popular with growers. Each stem can produce up to a dozen long-keeping purple flowers with bright white throats. It's an easy-blooming two-foot bifoliate that can be grown on bark. A pure white form is also available.

Hybrids—Cattleyas have been crossed with many other genera, such as *Brassavola*, *Laelia*, and *Sophronitis,* to produce an astonishing range of colorful and exotic hybrids.

Omnipresent Orchids

Orchids are the largest known family of plants in the world. They thrive on every continent except Antarctica and in almost every type of environment—from the cloud forests of the Andes to the near-desert of the Sahara. A handful are native to North America, including the Lady's Slipper, the state flower of Minnesota. Most of the true beauties, however, hail from the tropics.

CYMBIDIUM

Semiterrestrial by nature, cymbidiums are often seen in West Coast perennial gardens where the yearly temperatures range from 35 to 95 degrees F. They are also raised in large numbers for the cut-flower trade. Growing up to five feet tall, their upright sprays produce abundant amounts of long-lasting blooms in all shades of the spectrum—often in shocking combinations. Cymbidiums are robust plants with numerous fleshy roots, and seem to bloom better when confined to smaller pots. Cold night air encourages flowering spikes which at first are hard to distinguish from other vegetative growth. They appreciate year-round watering, a good breezy atmosphere, and should be fertilized regularly. Their name comes from *cymbid*, the Greek word for boat, and refers to their wide, flowering lip.

SELECTIONS

Hybrids outperform all species of cymbidiums in growing ease and overall beauty. There are two main hybrid types of cymbidiums:

STANDARD—Growing up to five feet tall, these hybrids sprout many three- to five-inch flowers. They enjoy bright sunlight and cool night temperatures, making them ideal low-maintenance outdoor plants for West Coast climates. There are many award-winning standard cymbidiums to choose from.

MINIATURE—Only one to two feet tall, these compact hybrids yield smaller flowers in many colors one to three inches across. Native to Japan and China, miniatures tolerate the heat better than standards.

Dendrobium

In Latin, *Dendrobium* translates as "living on trees" and that may be the only characteristic that binds the members of this large and diverse group. Native to many parts of Asia, the more than one thousand species of dendrobiums are found everywhere from hot and steamy lagoons to cool, breezy mountain tops. Some are evergreen, while others are deciduous requiring a seasonal resting period of low temperatures and minimal water. Stems are often bamboo-like in appearance. Small *Dendrobium* flowers come in shades of violet, rose, and yellow, many with brightly colored lips. The blooms are often borne on long, arching sprays. All seem to love light and usually benefit from a summer outing on the patio. They prefer being a bit root-bound. Miniature varieties are available.

Den. densiflorum—produces dramatic cascading sprays of up to a hundred tiny golden yellow flowers with frilly lips. A Nepalese native with thick, shiny leaves, it needs cool winter nights for best bloom.

Den. nobile—a fragrant orchid from India bearing small groups of brilliant white blooms with purple tips and maroon throats. A deciduous and hardy sun-lover that can tolerate swings in temperatures but needs cooler weather to stimulate blooming. Extensively hybridized.

Den. phalaenopsis—an Australian species that resembles *Phalaenopsis* in floral appearance and culture. Long-lasting flowers from white to deep red are borne on two parallel stems. Tall pseudobulbs characterize this easy-to-grow evergreen. Many hybrids are available.

Den. spectabile—a species from New Guinea with green, purple, and white twisted flowers. An easy-to-grow evergreen, best suited for intermediate to cool temperatures.

Hybrids: Stunning hybrids are available, including the Yamamoto series, developed at the Yamamoto nursery in Hawaii.

Fatal Attraction

Hawaiian honeybees have found an introduced Dendrobium *orchid to be alluring but deadly. When the bees feast on the flower's nectar they become lodged and die in the narrow blooms. In its native Asian home, the orchid poses no threat to the smaller indigenous bees that feed on its nectar.*

Oncidium

This large and colorful genus possesses long spikes of mostly brown and yellow flowers, but white, purple, green, and pink show up on occasion. The distinctive four-lobed flowers often resemble the head, arms, and ruffled skirts of peasant dancers, thus earning them the nickname of the dancing lady orchids. Native to many New World locales, they vary considerably in cultural requirements, but all appreciate bright light, strong breezes, and plenty of soakings with definite dry periods in between. They are generally easy to grow and adapt well to most homes. Some do best on slabs of oak bark, while others prefer basket or pot culture. Miniature types are available.

Selections

Onc. ampliatum—the large rounded pseudo-bulbs look like turtle shells in this species.

Four-foot arching sprays produce small, clear yellow flowers with white and red markings.

Onc. crispum—The large, coppery red, ruffled petals have a touch of yellow at the lip. This Brazilian native flowers in the fall or winter.

Onc. papilio—called the butterfly orchid due to its long, thin, modified petals and sepals. The ten- to fifteen-inch spikes can often produce yellow and brown flowers through the year.

Onc. sphacelatum—This species features robust pseudobulbs and two-foot leaves that yield dozens of spikes and hundreds of upright golden yellow and brown flowers.

Onc. splendidum—known as a "mule-ear" type, due to its short pseudobulbs. Three-foot leaves offer brown marked flowers with pronounced lemon yellow lips. Prefers full sun.

ODONTOGLOSSUM

Odontoglossums have been very popular in England since the first one crossed the Atlantic in the 18th century. Mild English summers suit these Andean epiphytes, as do the cloudy, cool climates found in New England and the Pacific Northwest. Distinctive flattened pseudobulbs send up spikes of eight to fifteen flowers. The ruffled-edged blooms of yellow, green, and white are often exquisitely decorated with contrasting touches of brown and pink. They enjoy plenty of indirect sun and lots of cool, moist, moving air. Don't allow them to become too dry before watering. Red streaks in the foliage are signs of a bit too much light, but this often has an invigorating effect on the flower. They thrive in crowded, humid conditions and should be repotted only if necessary.

Odont. crispum—a very beautiful Colombian species much improved through self-crosses. Small flowers range from pure white to rosy and are often dotted with specks of red or brown.

Odont. grande—known as the tiger orchid due to its yellow and brown bars and impressive bloom size. The half-dozen large, waxy flowers are elaborately sculpted and arise from foot-long stalks.

Odont. pulchellum—The small, white, fragrant flowers suggest its common name—the lily of the valley orchid. Compact in size, each stalk produces spikes of three to ten flowers with yellow and brown centers. Easy to grow.

Hybrids: *Vuylsterkeara* cambria 'Plush'—an intergeneric hybrid famous for its large flamboyant ruffled lip and intense burgundy color.

PAPHIOPEDILUM

The lady's slipper orchids are named for their prominent pouch-shaped lip and are famed for their other-worldly appearance. Their long-lasting, waxy blooms often look rubbery or artificial, but this only adds to their strange charm. The whitish, yellow, and green flowers of this genus are marked with spots of brown or maroon and have a prominently adorned dorsal sepal. The lower sepals are fused together and may be difficult to see. For all their bizarre looks, paphiopedilums (or paphs for short) are some of the easiest orchids to grow and are quite content to be on a windowsill or under lights. These Asian terrestrials are divided into two groups distinguished by their foliage. Green-leafed types require cooler temperatures and usually bloom in the winter. The mottled-leaf types are more intermediate in their temperature preferences and are summer bloomers. Both require subdued lighting, frequent watering, and gentle breezes. Paphs are very sensitive to fertilizers, so don't overfeed them, and remember to periodically flush the soil with pure water to remove accumulated salts. They enjoy summering outdoors and should be repotted in plastic pots every one or two years.

SELECTIONS

Paph. bellatulum—The attractively mottled foliage of these paphs yields single broad-petaled flowers on very short stems. The bloom is pale yellow to white with purplish-brown spots. Native to Burma and Thailand.

Paph. callosum—The large four-inch flowers sport a huge green and white top sepal streaked with purple. The petals are spotted with black, tipped in purple, with a prominent maroon lip. Leaves are mottled and are light blue-green in color. Spring and summer bloomer.

Paph. fairrieanum—a small, ornate paph with light green leaves. The prominent top sepal is white with purple netting. The ruffled petals curl upward and have tiny tufts of hair on their margins. The lip is greenish, with purple veins. Blooms in autumn.

Paph. insigne—a popular easy-to-grow paph that produces four- to five-inch apple green flowers with maroon spots. The lip is helmet-shaped, and the veined petals are long and twisted. This Himalayan species has many named varieties, and may bear two flowers per stem.

Paph. venustum—dark green, mottled leaves that are purple underneath make this a very attractive foliage plant. The heart-shaped dorsal sepal is white, streaked with green. Red-tipped petals are warty, with fine black hairs, and the lip is bronze, netted with heavy green veins.

Hybrids: A famously easy hybrid is the white and green *Paph.* Maudiae. Other *Paph.* Maudiae forms are red or burgundy. Most hybrids are grown from seeds, as mericloning techniques are still being perfected.

PHALAENOPSIS

Perhaps the perfect windowsill orchid, phalaenopsis (or phals for short) are easy to grow and hold their blooms for months. *Phalaina* means "moth" in Greek, and it's easy to see how they were named. Their delicately rounded flowers resemble a group of moths gracefully alighting upon an arched branch. Phal flowers come in many solids and stripes, and their foliage is often attractive shades of green-grays and silvers. Their need for light is minimal, and they will be quite content with a nice eastern exposure. That doesn't mean you can't keep them on brighter sills, but you may have to filter direct sunlight. These Asian natives also require higher humidity than is usual in most homes. Lacking water-storing pseudobulbs, they don't tolerate drying out. Water them during the day, and don't allow moisture to stand in the recesses of the crown. Monopodial in growth, older specimens may need to be topped and the upper portion repotted. For best performance repot every two or three years.

SELECTIONS

Phal. lueddemanniana—a small Philippine species that produces up to twenty two-inch, star-shaped flowers. Fragrant blooms are creamy white to purple, and are often tinged with pink, brown, or purple bars and spots. The lip is a brilliant carmine. Many hybrids available.

Phal. schilleriana—The best-known phal has dark green and gray mottled foliage. When in bloom, hundreds of two- to three-inch white-tinged pink flowers appear on large branching sprays. Its long, flattened roots have a wonderful silver sheen. Very easy to grow.

Phal. stuartiana—Similar to *P. schilleriana*, this species boasts many small white flowers with cinnamon spots on lower parts. A tiny horned lip is colored deep orange. Attractive gray and silver foliage with purple undersides. Many hybrids.

Phal. violacea—This very popular phal has fleshy, pale green flowers with rosy-purplish centers. Its fragrance is reminiscent of violets. The Malaysian form can appear solid purple or albino, and is often used in breeding. Requires deep shade and high humidity.

Hybrids: Many easy-to-grow hybrids are available that bloom in different months. By choosing carefully, you can have phals in flower year-round.

Vanda

Vandas are monopodial orchids from Asia with leathery leaves, strong aerial roots, and beautiful floral sprays. Their leaves can take the form of long, flattened straps or thin, upright pencils. The pencil-leafed forms require full sun. Although they grow slowly, vandas are long-living and can reach six or seven feet. If they get too big for their surroundings, the upper portion can be cut off and used to start a new plant. The flowers can reach six inches across, and come in a wide spectrum of colors, including purple, brown, red, white, and blue—all of which can be seen in the many patterned and spotted hybrids available. Vandas can tolerate hot weather, high humidity, and brief cold snaps, making them good choices for tropical patios. They need more water and fertilizer than most other orchids, and don't tolerate repotting well. For that reason, they are often grown in baskets which are simply dropped into bigger baskets as the plant grows.

SELECTIONS

V. coerulea—features spikes of five to fifteen pale to dark blue symmetrically shaped flowers with a distinct netting of dark veins. Widely hybridized; there are numerous cultivars available.

V. sanderiana—also called *Euanthe sanderiana*, features three- to four-inch flowers which display combinations of white, red, brown, and green. Fall flowering.

V. tricolor—also known as *V. suavis*, this hearty species bears white flowers with dark red spots and a vivid magenta lip.

Hybrids: There is a wide selection of excellent vandas available as hybrids, including the famous *V.* Rothschildiana, a cross of *V. coerulea* and *V. sanderiana*. Smaller and more colorful hybrids have resulted from *Vanda* crosses with other species.

BEST BETS FOR BEGINNERS

Paphiopedilums, phalaenopsis, and Cattleyas
are the three most recommended generas for
beginners to try, but don't stop there. More
orchids that have been proven on windowsills
across America are:

> *Ascocentrum curvifolium*
> *Brassavola nodosa*
> *Broughtonia sanguinea*
> *Cattleya guttata* 'Leopoldii'
> *Cattleya* Princess Bells
> *Chysis laevis*
> *Cymbidium* Ivy Fung 'Demke'
> *Dendrobium phalaenopsis*
> *Dendrobium* New Guinea
> *Encyclia* Mariae 'Greenlace'
> *Epidendrum atropurpureum*
> *Epidendrum fragrans*

Epidendrum radicans
Laelia flava
Laelia tenebrosa
Leptotes bicolor 'Karem'
Laeliocattleya Yung Hua 'Red Top'
Ludisia discolor
Lycaste aromatica 'Ivanhoe'
Lycaste skinneri 'Fertility Gardens'
Miltonia Evergreen Joy 'Carmen Cole'
Miltonia Goodhope Bay 'Raindrops'
Miltonia spectabilis
Odcdm. 'Tiger Hambuehren'
Odontia Chignik
Odontia grande
Oncidium Gower Ramsey
Oncidium sphacelatum
Oncidium Wilbur 'Elizabeth'
Paphiopedilum Bell O'Ireland

Paphiopedilum callosum
Paphiopedilum fairrieanum
Paphiopedilum Farnmoore 'Rex'
Paphiopedilum hirsutissimum
Paphiopedilum insigne
Paphiopedilum Maudiae
Paphiopedilum 'Niobe'
Paphiopedilum Orchilla 'Chilton'
Paphiopedilum spicerianum
Paphiopedilum sukhakulii
Paphiopedilum Wineva 'Superior'
Phalaenopsis schilleriana
Phalaenopsis stuartiana
Phragmipedium caudatum
Rhynchostylis gigantea
Slc. Jewel Box 'Black Magic' AM/AOS
Slc. Jewel Box 'Dark Waters'

MINIATURE ORCHIDS

If you're growing in a limited space, don't despair. There are a number of interesting orchids that stay under six inches. Look for some of these at specialty nurseries listed in the back of this book.

Aerangis (many species)
Ascocentrum miniatum
Brassavola nodosa
Cattleya walkeriana
Dendrobium aggregatum
Dendrobium linguiforme
Dendrobium loddigesii
Epidendrum polybulbon
Epidendrum porpax
Gastrochilus (many species)
Laelia pumila
Masdevallia triangularis

Neofinetia falcata
Ornithocephalus (many species)
Paphiopedilum bellatulum
Paphiopedilum concolor
Paphiopedilum godefroyae
Phalaenopsis equestris
Pleurothallis (many species)
Polystachya (many species)
Restrepia sanguinea
Sarcochilus hartmannii
Sophronitis (many species)
Stelis (many species)
Trichocentrum (many species)

MAKING SCENTS

Some orchids are as well known for their fragrances as they are for their beauty. The famous 'Lady-of-the-Night' orchid (*Brassavola nodosa*) is famous for its special nocturnal perfume. Because fragrance is used to attract not only orchid growers but pollinating insects, a few orchids emit less pleasant odors. *Cirrhopetalum graveolans* brings in flies with its smell of rotten meat. Listed here are a few better-smelling orchids along with their fragrances:

Phalaenopsis schilleriana—rose
Oncidium lawrencianum—carnation
Phalaenopsis lueddemanniana—vanilla
Oncidium Sharry Baby—chocolate
Rhyncholaelia digbyana—lemon
Laelia purpurata—licorice

Vanda tricolor—candy
Acineta superba—sandalwood
Neofinetia falcata—gardenia
Zygopetalum mackayi—lilac
Epidendrum alatum—angelica
Odontoglossum (many)—cinnamon
Odontoglossum blande—honey
Encyclia citrina—citrus

Orchid with a Twist, Please
A nutritious beverage called "salep" is brewed
from orchid tubers in the Middle East. It is
also thought to have aphrodisiac powers.

The Envelope, Please

Glance at any orchid catalog and you're sure to see some listings followed by a series of letters such as FCC/AOS or AM/RHS. These suffixes indicate awards bestowed upon flowers of exceptional quality by one of several orchid societies. Highly coveted, these awards are granted for superior forms, hybrid improvements, trends, and even exceptional growing skills. The American Orchid Society (AOS) presents the following awards:

For Hybrid and Species flowers

FCC = First Class Certificate; the highest award for scores of 90–100 points

AM = Award of Merit; for flowers scoring 80–89 points

HCC = Highly Commended Certificate; for flowers scoring 75–79 points

For Species Flowers Only

CBR = Certificate of Botanical Recognition; for rare and unusual species

CHM = Certificate of Horticultural Merit; for well-grown species

For Outstanding Specimen Plants

CCM = Certificate of Cultural Merit; awarded to a grower of any level of expertise for an excellent plant bearing large numbers of superb flowers

Other societies presenting similar awards include: the Royal Horticultural Society (RHS), the South Florida Orchid Society (SFOS), and the Honolulu Orchid Society (HOS).

GLOSSARY

aerial root—a root growing in the air

AOS—American Orchid Society

backbulb—an older pseudobulb that no longer bears leaves

bifoliate—having two leaves

cultivar—a selected form of a species or hybrid

epiphyte—a plant that grows on another plant but does not feed from it

flasking—method of germinating seeds in a laboratory

genus—subdivision of a family; plural is genera

grex—a group of progeny from a cross between two plants

hybrid—an artificial cross between two plants of different species or genera

intergeneric—between two or more genera

keiki—an offshoot of a mature plant; Hawaiian for "baby"

labellum—the modified lip or lowest petal of an orchid flower

lithophyte—a plant that grows on rocks

mericlone—a clone produced from meristem tissue

monopodial—new growth arising from the top of the plant

multigeneric—involving more than one genera

pseudobulb—the thickened, fleshy stem base of some orchids

sepals—the outermost parts of the orchid flower

species—subdivision of a genus

species orchid—an unhybridized orchid from nature

spike—a stem bearing many flowers

sympodial—new growth arising from rhizomes

terrestrial—a plant that grows in the ground

unifoliate—having one leaf

variety—subdivision of a species singled out for specific qualities

velamen—the spongy covering of many orchid roots

SOURCES

THE AMERICAN ORCHID SOCIETY

Based in West Palm Beach, Florida, the American Orchid Society (AOS) is one of the largest plant societies in the world, with a membership of more than 27,000. Their exquisite full-color monthly publication, the *AOS Bulletin*, is full of articles on orchid growing and breeding and has a useful advertising section in the back. The AOS also sponsors orchid shows, judging, and awards, in addition to working with hundreds of local affiliates throughout the U.S. and Canada. An extensive line of books and videos are also available.

Yearly membership includes a subscription to the *Bulletin*, a copy of the useful *Growing Orchids*, the *AOS Almanac* listing clubs and events, a book list, and other benefits.

The American Orchid Society
6000 South Olive Avenue
West Palm Beach, FL 33405
(407) 585-8666 phone
(407) 585-0654 fax

LOCAL HEROES

A great place to buy plants is from a nearby greenhouse that specializes in orchids. You can find these in the telephone directory (under "Orchids" or "Greenhouses") or by asking at garden centers. Many of these greenhouses belong to passionate hobbyists rather than commercial growers, so they may be a little tough to track down; but visiting a local greenhouse gives you a chance to look at varieties in person, and also provides an opportunity to talk to a knowledgeable grower about what plants are best suited for your home. Your local orchid club may also offer plant sales or swap meets where orchids (and advice) come cheap. Buying locally eliminates the stress and costs of shipping, but avoid purchasing from plant stores that don't specialize in orchids. You'll likely end up with a second-rate plant at an inflated price. Begin by purchasing mature plants. These are orchids that have bloomed at least once and will most likely bloom again.

Orchid Fiction

The great fictional detective, Nero Wolfe, raised orchids in the rooftop greenhouse of his Manhattan brownstone; H. G. Wells wrote a short story about a man-eating orchid; and comic-strip heroine Brenda Starr's mysterious husband, Basil, needed a black orchid serum in order to live.

MAIL-ORDER ORCHIDS

Once you feel more confident in your growing abilities, you may want to buy new plants via the wide world of orchids-by-mail. There are dozens of fine nurseries across the country that offer everything from native species to hybrids with pedigrees as long as your arm. The catalogs range from simple photocopied lists to full-color publications with gorgeous photographs. The sources listed here have especially colorful or interesting catalogs:

Carter and Holmes Orchids
629 Mendenhall Road
P.O. Box 668
Newberry, SC 29108
(803) 276-0579

Everglades Orchids
1101 Tabit Road
Belle Glade, FL 33430
(407) 996-9600

H&R Nurseries, Inc.
41-240 Hihimanu Street
Waimanalo, HI 96795
(808) 259-9626

J&L Orchids
20 Sherwood Road
Easton, CT 06612
(203) 261-3772

Kawamoto Orchid Nursery
2630 Waiomao Road
Honolulu, HI 96816
(808) 732-5808

Orchids by Hausermann
2N 134 Addison Road
Villa Park, IL 60181-1191
(708) 543-6855

Orchids Limited
4630 Fernbrook Lane
Plymouth, MN 55446
(612) 559-6425

Penn Valley Orchids
239 Old Gulph Road
Wynnewood, PA 19096
(610) 642-9822

RF Orchids
28100 S.W. 182nd Avenue
Homestead, FL 33030-1804
(305) 245-4570

Stewart Orchids
3376 Foothill Road
P.O. Box 550
Carpinteria, CA 93013
(805) 684-5448

Zuma Canyon Orchids
5949 Bonsall Drive
Malibu, CA 90265
(310) 457-9771

BOOKS

All About Growing Orchids
Ortho Books, 1988

Home Orchid Growing
Rebecca T. Northen, 1990

Orchids Simplified
Henry Jaworski, 1992

Orchids
Peter Arnold, 1994

Orchids
Joyce Stewart, 1988

Orchids
Sunset Books, 1977

The World Wildlife Book of Orchids
Jack Kramer, 1989

ORCHID COLLECTIONS YOU CAN VISIT

Longwood Gardens, Kennett Square, DE

Missouri Botanical Gardens , St. Louis, MO

The Brooklyn Botanical Gardens, Brooklyn, NY

The Royal Botanical Gardens at Kew, Kew, England